P9-CSA-566

THE WEEKEND CRAFTER
Painting Ceramics

THE WEEKEND CRAFTER

Painting Ceramics

Easy Projects and Stylish Designs to Paint in a Weekend

M O I R A   N E A L

A N D   L Y N D A   H O W A R T H

Lark
Books

First published in the USA by
Lark Books, 50 College St., Asheville, NC 28801

Distributed by Random House, Inc. in the United States and Canada

Library of Congress Cataloging-in-Publication Data Available

Originally published in 1999 by New Holland Publishers (UK) Ltd

Copyright © 1999 New Holland Publishers (UK) Ltd.
All rights reserved.

Editor: **Gillian Haslam**
Designer: **Peter Crump**
Photographer: **Shona Wood**

Editorial Direction: **Yvonne McFarlane**

To Amelia, Edward, Claire and Gareth –
may the Union Bars flourish with our royalties!

The written instructions, photographs, designs, patterns, and projects
in this volume are intended for the personal use of the reader and may
be reproduced for that purpose only. Any other use, especially
commercial use, is forbidden under law without written permission
of the copyright holder.

Every effort has been made to ensure that all the information in this
book is accurate. However, due to differing conditions, tools, and
individual skills, the publishers cannot be responsible for any injuries,
losses, or other damages which may result from the use of the
information in this book.

Printed in Malaysia

All rights reserved

ISBN 1-57990-090-9

CONTENTS

INTRODUCTION

It all started when we were sunning ourselves in the garden on a hot summer's day, looking forward to seeing the first copy of our previous book in this series, *Painting Glass in a Weekend*, when we suddenly decided it was time for a new challenge. On such a hot day most normal people would be dreaming of diving into a cool swimming pool or having a water fight. Thankfully all you compulsive craft workers reading this will completely understand our need to get motoring on a new challenge. Having had so much fun writing our glass painting book, we simply could not wait any longer before embarking on this new project.

We discovered that painting ceramics can be even more fun than glass because the opacity of china allows you to achieve completely different results and, in the case of bowls, cups, mugs and so on, there are two surfaces to paint instead of one. Now you can paint a range of china to match your hand-decorated glassware. The other exciting development is the availability of new paints which are both washable *and* completely food-safe which takes the craft into a new dimension. All you need is a domestic oven and your items can be patterned for life.

It is always great fun to be creative and find new ways of doing things, but while trying our various designs for this book we became very frustrated at being unable to paint perfect concentric circles on our china. In desperation we resorted to using Tony's hifi ... he was out at the time! The results were brilliant, but for some reason he failed to share our enthusiasm and was most relieved when Jim appeared with an ancient record player which is now well splattered with paint!

The only problem with china painting is that it does become compulsive, particularly when there are two of you egging each other on, and much practice and experimentation is required on anything and everything you can lay your hands on. We had to laugh during a recent painting session. Jim came into the kitchen to make some coffee and exclaimed, 'Hang on ... this was just an ordinary cup and saucer the other day'. Yes, this is true. The cup and saucer he was talking about now take pride of place between these pages and can never be referred to as ordinary again.

We hope that you will enjoy our book and that you too will no longer have cupboards full of ordinary china, but bursting with colorful creations that you will be proud to own. When the shelves start to overflow with your designer china, which they surely will, you will know it is time to start wrapping them up and giving them away as presents.

Have fun!

Moira Neal.

Lynda Howarth

Moira and Lynda, partners in design

GETTING STARTED

Like so many crafts, all that painting on ceramics requires is some basic equipment, lots of enthusiasm and a willingness to try something new. You will find the projects featured in this book are all quite straightforward, but take a moment first to read through this chapter which explains the various techniques involved. We have developed several new techniques for you to try and the majority of them do not require any special ability. Rest assured that it really won't be long before you are ready to try the projects. Once you have followed a few of them, allow your own creative powers to take over and develop your own designs and color combinations.

CERAMIC PAINTING PRODUCTS

There are many ceramic paints now available. They fall into several categories:

1 Water-based paints which do not need baking and are ideal for items which are not going to be washed. They are also perfect for children to use, although children should be supervised at all times.

2 Water-based paints which need to be baked at 390°F (200°C) for 30 minutes. Items decorated with this type of paint must be washed by hand. The colors are bright and dense and easy to apply.

3 New generation water-based paints which are baked at 300°F (150°C) and are said to have good dishwasher resistance. These are ideal for tableware

EQUIPMENT AND MATERIALS

Apart from the paints and brushes, you will probably find that you already have much of the equipment listed here. There are several different types of ceramic paints now on the market (see right). These will be available either in your local craft or hobby shop, or via mail order (see page 78 for suppliers).

The other obvious requirement is a good supply of china. You will probably need to have a few practice runs before tackling your first project, so acquire a collection of plain china at boot fairs, garage sales and charity shops for trying out new paints and different techniques. Always wash the china in hot soapy water to remove any dust or grease before painting.

Additional useful items include rubber resist paint, rubber shaper brushes for etching, aerosol glue and an old record player (useful and fun if you fancy being creative!). Refer to page 11 for more details on this unusual painting method.

A selection of china
Ceramic paints (see right for more details)
White spirit (if using solvent-based paints)
Good quality paintbrushes in a variety of sizes; see individual projects (good brushes are quite expensive but a worthwhile investment, so put them on your birthday or Christmas wish list)
Container for water or white spirit
Outliners compatible with the paints being used
Palette or plate for mixing colors
Kitchen paper towels
Toothpicks
Cotton swabs
Sponges of various densities and textures
Masking tape
Scissors
Paper
Chinagraph pencil
Newspaper to protect your worksurface
Apron
Domestic oven (if using oven-bake paints)

TIP

To keep the mess down, once you are ready to begin, protect your workspace with layers of old newspaper or an old tablecloth as some of the ceramic paints are solvent-based and may damage some surfaces.

If children are going to help with the painting, make sure they are also well covered up.

SAFETY NOTES

There is no reason why children cannot enjoy the hobby of ceramic painting as well as adults. Make sure that they are supervised at all times and choose water-based paints for them to use. Store paints and brush cleaner in a cool place, well out of the reach of prying hands when not in use.

Always follow manufacturers' specific instructions regarding the baking process if it is required (see facing page for more details).

A collection of china ready for painting. Broken or unwanted items can be used as test pieces.

OUTLINING

There are various types of outliner on the market and it is important to select one compatible with the paint you are using. If using an oven-bake paint, the outliner must be the same.

Outliners are slightly tricky to use at first and so it is worth practicing to perfect your technique. Have a piece of kitchen towel to hand to wipe the tip clean before you begin. You will find that very little pressure is required and the aim is to produce an even finish. The projects show that outliners may be used to produce a variety of finishes to your work. Photographs ① and ② show how their application onto basic painted shapes, such as the plate, or masked off areas can be very effective.

and glasses and we have used them extensively in this book. They are available in a huge range of colors, both transparent and opaque, and once baked feel wonderfully smooth. Practice may be needed with these, as indeed all paints, to achieve the density of cover required. It is often better to sponge on two light coats, allowing the first to dry before applying the second. There is a matt medium in the range which, if used alone, gives a wonderful frosted effect. Used with the other colors in the range as instructed, it gives a matt finish without affecting the color. Items painted this way must be fully baked to ensure good adhesion of the color and a more permanent design.

4 Solvent-based paints which are perfect to use on china not intended for food use and may be hand-washed with extreme care. They are available as transparent or opaque shades and are quick drying. Brushes need to be cleaned using a compatible solvent, generally white spirit. These paints are flammable and should not be used near a naked flame nor should children use them unsupervised. Make sure your work area is well ventilated and well protected with plenty of newspaper.

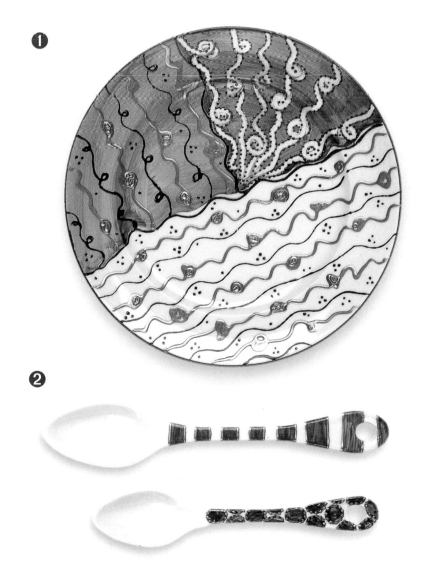

❶

❷

3

They may be used on their own to produce a series of dots, stitch effects, solid and broken lines and cross hatching as well as in conjunction with paints to give emphasis or detail to a design ③.

PAINTBRUSHES

We have been busy experimenting with different types of paintbrush and have been delighted with the results. It is certainly well worth investing in a new brush occasionally. A good quality brush gives the best results and here we tell you about some really useful types.

• **WIDE, FLAT PAINTBRUSHES**
Here is the perfect way to create broad even bands of color on your china. These brushes are available in a number of sizes but we have found the 2 cm (¾ in) brush to be the most useful. A tartan effect is easily achieved by laying on bands of color and then overlaying in the opposite direction with the same or contrasting colors ①. Allow plenty of time for the first color to dry before applying the next. Later, fine lines may be added using a conventional paintbrush or outliner. Look in the tile gallery on pages 40-41 for some more ideas.

This type of brush may also be used to produce a series of parallel lines which looks very effective. A simple daisy type floral design is made by painting five or six lines in a circle, leaving the center free to paint in a different color. A number of different shades could be used to build up a more sophisticated type of flower design, depending on your confidence and the effect you want.

• **FAN HEADED PAINTBRUSHES**
These are very useful items for edging plates in the 1930s' style with feathery brush strokes ②. Load the brush very lightly with paint and flick the brush from the outside of the plate towards the center, making the strokes as long or short as you wish. This is also a good way to achieve a grass effect.

1

2

Contemporary swirls are easy to paint, too, by lightly rotating the brush on the surface, from just a few turns to a full 360 degree swirl.

3

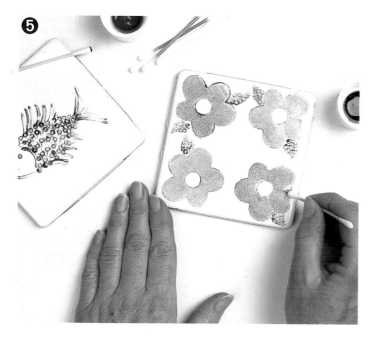

• **ANGLED PAINTBRUSHES**
These provide yet another simple way to apply paint in an interesting way. We have used this type of brush to edge tiles in the gallery and also to finish the edge of the bowl on page 34. One, two or more colors may be used alternately to produce an interesting edge. It is also very easy to paint chevron stripes with this brush ③.

A good, long angled dagger brush can give a perfect leaf or petal shape with just one stroke and a little practice to get the angle right ④.

• **COTTON SWABS**
These can also be used for painting ⑤. The tip holds sufficient paint to be able to draw simple outline shapes, such as the fish shape shown. They are perfect too for painting leaves and frondy

seaweed. Cotton swabs are also ideal to use for making one or a series of dots in the center of a flower for example. They produce an interesting texture and can be used to create geometric shapes such as diamonds, crosses and squares made up of a row of dots. The lamp base project on page 44 has been partially decorated with this method. Try combining painting and dotting together. If the cotton swabs are used on freshly applied paint, they may be used to create etched designs and to add etched detailing, to a leaf for example.

RECORD PLAYER PAINTING

Here is a great idea for those of you who are feeling adventurous. As well as being fun, it is a practical method of applying paint evenly to a circular object and works very well on a plate. Find an old record player for this – not a 78 r.p.m. as you will have no control at all! Scrunch up some tin foil into a circle which will fit around the central metal knob on the record deck and then lay the plate on top. Turn the record player on to a slow speed and take time to centralize the plate. Apply the paint to the plate with a large soft brush or sponge until it is evenly covered. If you wish to etch into it, do this immediately with a cotton swab, rubber shaper brush or finger. See the plate gallery on page 56 for examples of this technique.

ETCHING

This is a very good way to add emphasis without having to use another color ①. It is perfect for adding details like leaves, feathers, scales on fish, eyes and so on as well as creating abstract designs on a sponged surface. You will need to etch the design as soon as the paint has been applied.

Use a toothpick for very fine designs or for details on tiny items. A cotton swab or typist's pencil-style rubber, which may be sharpened with a knife or pencil sharpener depending on the effect required, are both ideal for chunkier etching ②. There are some wonderful new rubber-tipped 'shaper' brushes on the market now specially designed for etching which we have found very useful.

need to resort to thin paper or specialist adhesive stencilling film which will mould more easily to the contours of the china and can be used several times.

You can make your own stencils by photocopying your chosen pattern first. Paper is fine for one-off designs, otherwise use adhesive mount to attach the pattern to the card you are using and allow the glue to dry for about ten minutes before attempting to cut it. Protect your worksurface with a cutting mat or a thick layer of old newspaper before you start. Use a metal ruler as a guide for cutting straight lines and avoid trying to cut around angular designs in one go.

USING YOUR STENCILS

Lightly spray the back of the stencil with aerosol spray mount to hold it in place. On cylindrical items you may also need to secure it with a couple of elastic bands, too.

Pour a little ceramic paint into a saucer or the lid of the pot of paint and use a piece of old sponge to apply the paint ②. It is always worth

STENCILLING

This is a good way to decorate china with a regular repeat pattern or a single bold design. It is particularly useful if you intend to sell your ceramics as it is a very quick process once the initial stencil cutting is out of the way.

It is worth taking great care at the beginning in order to get good, professional results and the initial investment in a craft knife or scalpel and spare blades is worthwhile ①. For one-off stencils to decorate on flat surfaces, thin card or even a good quality paper is ideal. If you are using the stencil on a curved surface, you may

experimenting at this stage. Natural sponge will give a coarser, more rustic look than synthetic sponge which gives a more even finish.

Torn paper stencils can be very effective and are quick and easy to make ③. For example, to make a heart simply fold the paper in half and then draw the shape on as a tearing guide. Carefully tear along the drawn line, then open out and use as above.

MASKING AND REVERSE STENCILLING

There are several ways to mask areas of china before sponging. Stick on shapes like stars, hearts, ring reinforcements or indeed any shape you care to cut out. Use aerosol adhesive mount to apply your own shapes. This method can also be used to add a regular pattern to the edge of a plate for example. Masking tape, torn strips of paper and very thin tape available from art shops can also be used ④. Squares, oblongs, stripes of varying widths and harlequin designs are all possible this way. The masked off area can later be embellished with outliner to add relief pattern, such as veining on a leaf.

For a checkered effect, simply stick lines of low-tack tape onto the china. Sponge the gaps with several colors and then allow to dry completely before removing the tape and reapplying it in the opposite direction and repeating the process. Clean up any rough paint edges with a scalpel.

MASKING FLUID

Rubber solution masking fluid is a very useful addition to your kit ⑤. Use an old paintbrush to paint it over a ready marked design. (Wash the brush immediately to prevent it being ruined.) Allow the fluid to dry for a full 24 hours before being tempted to paint or sponge over it. When the paint has dried, use the tip of a toothpick to remove the rubber mask. If used over chinagraph, the marks will be removed with the rubber solution.

SAFETY NOTE

Dispose of broken and worn scalpel blades safely by wrapping in cardboard or placing in an old film canister.

STAMPING

A mosaic effect is very simple to achieve by cutting up thin kitchen sponge into squares and then lightly dipping into paint. Also try some of the many commercially available stamps too. These are ideal when working on a flat surface ①. Apply the paint to the stamp with a brush.

Potato printing is great fun and children will especially enjoy doing this. Cut out simple shapes from the potato to make repeat patterns and use biscuit (cookie) cutters to cut larger shapes like trees, hearts, stars and so on. The finished effect is fairly rustic but worth experimenting with ②.

SPONGING

Sponging is a quick and easy way to apply ceramic paints and a variety of finishes can be achieved. Practice on an old tile first. Anything from natural sponge to make-up sponges or thin sponge dishcloths can be used. Natural sponge gives a coarse, rustic effect, while synthetic sponge results in a finer finish. A graduated effect is made by gradually decreasing the pressure on the sponge as you work down the object or around the rim of a plate. A multicolored, graduated finish is achieved by using several colors in succession, allowing each one to merge into the next ③.

TIP

Thin sponge dishcloths are ideal as they can be cut into small pieces and thrown away after use. Wash them thoroughly before use to remove any coating.

We had fun sponging large dots with commercially available sponges; a similar effect can be made by cutting sponge into a circle.

You can either use paint straight from the pot or tip a little onto a saucer which has been covered in cling film first to make the cleaning up process quicker and easier.

PRINTING WITH LEAVES

Fresh leaves may also be used to take a print from. Use a sponge to apply a very small amount of paint to the veined reverse side of the leaf, then lay it in place on the china and press over it with damp cloth. Peel off the leaf immediately, taking care not to smudge the paint.

Use a range of green shades, or autumnal browns, rusts and a touch of gold for a stunning result. The edge of a plate decorated in this way could be sponged with gold. You could add berries painted freehand in bright red.

COLORWASHING

For this technique, paint is thinned down slightly and applied with a large soft brush ①. Stipple the paint on and merge colors into each other to produce a soft watercolor effect 'canvas' on which to base your design. Once the colorwash is completely dry, detailed painting may be worked on top as in the Dufy style jug on page 26.

CLEANING OFF UNWANTED PAINT BEFORE BAKING

It can be difficult to wash off the paints once they have dried but the quickest method is to wear rubber gloves and make up a hot solution of dishwasher detergent. Allow the object to soak for a few minutes and the design will wash off very easily.

TRANSFERRING DESIGNS

Unlike glassware, where the design is so easy to tape on the inside and to trace through, transferring onto china needs more thought. One way is to trace the design onto paper ② with a soft 2 or 3B pencil, then turn the paper over and tape in place on the surface of the china. Draw over design on the reverse side of the paper and the outline will be lightly transferred onto the china ③. Chinagraph pencils may also be used to mark out design but we have been careful to use chinagraph as a guide only as it may act as a resist if you try to paint over it. It will also show through light colors.

You can re-size any of the designs we have provided in the back of this book with a photocopier in order to tailor the size to your own china.

EMBELLISHMENTS

There are many ways in which to embellish your china but much depends upon how washable it needs to be. Shiny glass nuggets may be used to give a rich jewel-like finish to an exotic vase, for example, and should be held in place with a two-part or specialist glass glue. Sequins are easy to apply and come in a multitude of shapes and colors. The addition of cellophane wrapping and a pretty bow make your object into a very presentable gift.

INSPIRATION FOR DESIGNS

Wallpapers and borders, wrapping paper, gift cards, coloring books, curtain fabrics, and flower and bulb catalogues are good sources of inspiration. Do remember, however, that you may not sell any work using other people's designs.

For a baby gift you could use the nursery wallpaper design to inspire the design on the edge of a picture frame. Glasses, jugs and carafes decorated to match existing crockery or table linen make excellent gifts for adults and may be themed to celebrate a special occasion such as a special birthday or anniversary. If you are looking for ideas for floral designs, seek out fabrics, handkerchiefs and decorated papers as well as gardening magazines.

If you enjoy museums, why not visit one and get inspiration from old china? We found some fascinating pieces and there are so many styles that may be used for inspiration. The brightly colored Clarice Cliff designs can inspire your own ideas based on similar colors and simple shapes. Old Moorcroft pottery with its beautiful raised texture can be emulated by piping on outliner to give an extra dimension. Be sure never to copy anything exactly. Instead, loosely base your designs on what you have seen, taking shapes from different sources. This ensures that your work will always be original.

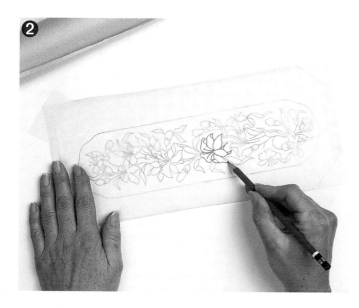

PROJECTS AND GALLERIES
FOR PAINTING CERAMICS

HARVEST TABLEWARE

Here is a really simple project to get you started on ceramic painting. We have used a set of embossed tableware which features apples, figs, grapes and plums but if you cannot find the same china, simply use the idea shown here to embellish any type of fruits, shading them as shown. This project is designed to look hand-painted, so don't worry if your brush strokes show.

1 Wash the china in hot soapy water. Then pick out the apples with the scarlet paint, painting one side rosier than the other for a realistic ripening effect and graduating the paint so that it fades towards the middle.

YOU WILL NEED

Embossed tableware either matching or assorted

Oven-bake enamel glaze such as Porcelaine 150 paints in scarlet 06, Havana 34 (brown), garnet 11, amethyst 13, peridot green 30 (olive) and green-gold 31

No 2 sable brush

Kitchen paper towel

Small bowl of water

TIP

If you want to vary the colors, be sure to use the transparent paints from the range. You may find it useful to keep all the paints out while you are working as you will need to mix the paints as you go along, moving them around you as you work.

VARIATIONS

Why not paint a set of embossed glasses to complete your set? The same oven-bake paints can be used to paint on glass too.

2 Fill in the apples and plums with Havana. Then, working clockwise if you are right-handed, paint the twisted rope edging with the same paint, wiping any excess paint off the brush with a piece of paper towel if necessary. You do not need to clean the brush.

3 Dip the brush into the garnet and pick out the figs. Also paint the grapes using the garnet, then clean the brush in the water and dab it dry on the paper towel.

4 Use amethyst paint to build up the color of the grapes and to add the shadows to the other fruits where they touch. Change the water, if necessary.

5 Working clockwise, paint the foliage using peridot green, applying the color slightly unevenly to add an impression of depth. Darken the centers of the leaves and add the veins to finish the natural look. Use the green-gold to add highlights to the leaves. Leave the crockery to dry for 24 hours and then bake it following manufacturer's instructions.

COLORWASHED COOKIE JAR

This is a wonderful free technique which could be applied to a multitude of surfaces. Enlarge or reduce the design to suit the size of the object being decorated. We have also decorated a jug to match.

1 Wash the jar in hot soapy water. Load a number 4 brush with water and then dip the tip into the first of the four colors. Apply the color with a very free, washy technique making it more dense in the center of each area. Repeat on the lid.

YOU WILL NEED

White cookie jar or other white china washed in hot soapy water

Oven-bake enamel glaze such as Porcelaine 150 paints in ruby 07, citrine 01 (yellow), emerald green 19, lapis blue 16, petroleum blue 22 (blue-black) and abyss 41 (very dark blue)

No 4 paintbrush

No 1 fine liner brush

Small bowl of water

Kitchen paper towels

Template (see page 70)

Sheet of cellophane

VARIATIONS

This technique can easily be adapted and used as a springboard for your own ideas. You may prefer to apply the colorwash all over as we have done on the adjacent jug.

2 Continue with the other colors, spacing them out to fill the surface. Leave some areas of white as we have or merge the colors into each other until you have a base you are happy to work on.

3 It is useful to practice the designs provided by laying a sheet of cellophane over them and following the lines using the fine liner brush. This type of brush makes it easier to produce long, sweeping strokes. If you are not too confident with your painting ability, it is a good idea to bake the jar at this stage for about 15 minutes, following the manufacturer's instructions. This will be long enough to 'set' the base coat so that any mistakes may be safely washed off.

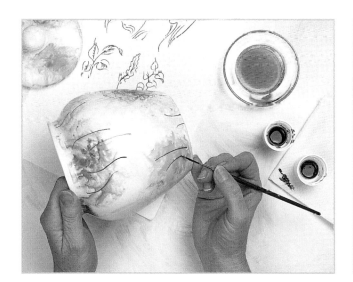

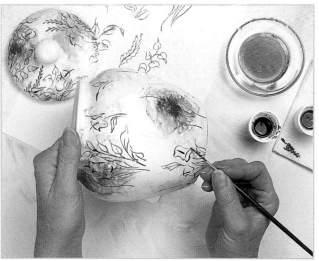

4 When you are ready to commit the pattern to the cookie jar, start by painting a skeleton of long, sweeping lines to represent plant stems, distributing them around the jar. Leave some of the white areas free from design.

5 Now add leaves and flowers using all six varieties shown on the template. Work freely and confidently to achieve a really flowing finish. Once you are happy with the result, leave to dry for 24 hours, then bake following the manufacturer's instructions.

BARGE-WARE POT

Black china provides the ideal background for this colorful paint technique. Here we have used acrylic deco paints for a greater density of color. These are water-resistant when dry and can withstand occasional, careful hand-washing. The beauty of this style of painting is its flexibility and the way the different roses, leaves and little flowers may be arranged to suit the container you are working on.

1 As brush strokes are an integral part of this design, it is worth taking time to practice each stage of the design first. Build up the petals of the red, yellow and white roses by starting with the central petals and working outwards with sweeping brush strokes.

YOU WILL NEED

Black china
Pattern (see page 71)
Tile or plate to practice on
Acrylic paints such as Pébéo Deco in red 06, yellow 03, blue 12, antique green 28 and white 41
No 2 paintbrush
Small bowl of water
Kitchen paper towels

VARIATIONS

Use this painting style to recycle old tinware as well as ceramics. It is traditionally used to decorate kettles, teapots, watering cans and tinware plates. The background for the design should be red, bottle green, navy or black.

2 Next, paint the little blue flowers with five dots of paint each. The pattern is flexible enough to adapt at this stage as long as you keep it roughly symmetrical in character with the traditional look.

3 Now paint the leaves with two brush strokes each. Again, practice this technique on the tile first. The definition is added at a later stage when the paint has completely dried.

4 Add definition to the small flowers by outlining with the white. While you have white on the brush, add the tiny white dots around the outside of the leaves and then paint the stamens on the red roses.

5 Paint the centers of the little flowers with the red along with the stamens on the white and yellow roses. Add the yellow brush strokes to the leaves and a few random brush strokes to the background to fill in any spaces. Wash out all brushes very thoroughly as acrylic paint can spoil them if allowed to dry. Leave the pot to dry for several days to allow the paint to harden completely before being tempted to use it.

JAZZ JUG

Capture the simple style of the 1950s with this stylized design. Stripes of various widths are decorated with simple outlines of musical notes, treble clefs and a variety of different instruments which are characteristic of the beatnik era.

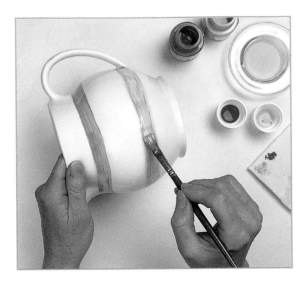

1 We mixed the Ming blue with a little ivory to soften the color slightly before we started. Using the flat wash brush, paint bands of blue and green onto the jug. The number of bands and their thickness is variable and will depend upon the size of your jug and the effect you want. Also paint a band of color down the handle.

YOU WILL NEED

Ceramic jug
Oven-bake enamel glaze such as Porcelaine 150 paints in Ming blue 1 (Chinese blue), ivory 43, opaline green 24 (dark seafoam green) and abyss blue 41 (very dark blue)
1 cm (⅜ in) flat brush
Dagger paintbrush or no 4 paintbrush
Fine liner paintbrush
Template (see page 71)
Old tile or plate to practice on
Kitchen paper towels
Container of water
Scalpel

VARIATIONS

Instead of a musical theme, you could choose to use simple trees and flowers or birds and fishes.

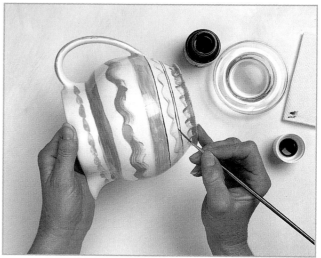

2 Next, add some wiggly lines with a dagger brush if you have one. If not, a similar effect is possible if you use a no 4 paintbrush. We have used just two colors for our jug but you may want more and now is a good time to add a third color if you wish. Soft pink would work well with the colors we have used.

3 Use a fine liner brush and the dark paint to place a few fine lines in between the others. You could use black outliner if you prefer, although this would give a far heavier feel to the jug.

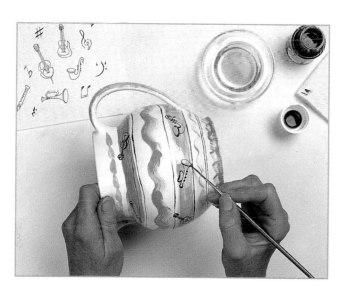

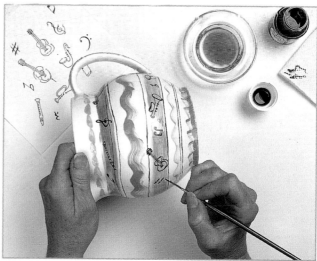

4 We have provided a number of musical notes and instruments to copy. There is no need to use them all and the ones you choose will depend on your artistic ability to copy them! We suggest you practice first on a tile or plate before applying them to the jug. If you wish to use any of the instruments, paint them at this stage. If you are nervous about making a mistake, simply bake the jug for about 20 minutes according to the manufacturer's instructions. This will set the surface well enough to wash off any errors.

5 Fill in some of the gaps with simple musical notes and signs but be careful not to over-complicate the design. If there are any irregularities in your work that you are not happy with, simply use a scalpel to neaten them up. Finally, once you are happy with your work, allow the jug to dry for 24 hours, then bake according to the manufacturer's instructions.

OLIVE DISH

The addition of a few sprays of olives has transformed this simple partitioned dish into a stylish piece of tableware perfect for serving olives, nuts, crisps and other nibbles. It would also make a very welcome gift for any occasion.

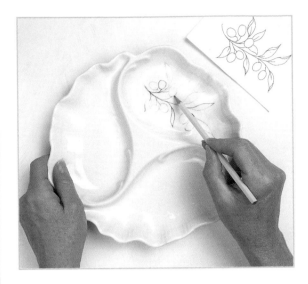

1 Wash the dish in hot soapy water before you begin. Use a pencil to copy the pattern onto the dish. If you are a confident painter you may not need to do this and simply have the pattern beside you to use as a guide as you work.

YOU WILL NEED

Partitioned dish

Template (see page 72)

Pencil

No 1 fine liner paintbrush

Oven-bake enamel glaze such as Porcelaine 150 paints in mummy brown 39 (dark brown), peridot 30 (olive), bronze 28 (leaf green), green-gold 31 and amethyst 13

Old tile or plate, for mixing paint

Kitchen paper towels

Small bowl of water

VARIATIONS

We have decorated a similar dish with holly. See the Christmas gallery on page 66 for further details.

2 Next, with the fine liner brush and the dark brown, paint the stalks of each of the three olive sprays. Use long flowing brush strokes working from the bottom of the spray upwards.

3 Before you start painting the leaves, make an olive green by mixing the two greens and a touch of brown. Paint the leaves with this mixture, working towards the tip of each one.

4 Now work into the leaves, extending the center stem definition with the brown. To make the leaves appear folded in places, run a light coat of brown paint down the edge of each leaf.

5 Make a mix of the amethyst and brown and use this to paint the olives. Apply the color fairly thinly working from the outside of each olive to achieve the characteristic shine. Allow the dish to dry for 24 hours, then bake following the manufacturer's instructions.

MARBLED PLATTER

The technique shown here allows you to imitate the fine detail of marble and produces a very realistic result. It could be applied to a variety of different surfaces in any one of the many marble colors produced in nature. This platter is ideal for serving cheese and biscuits or tarts and flans.

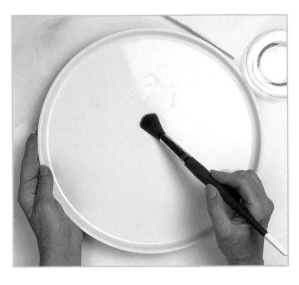

1 Wash the platter in hot soapy water. With the large wash brush or sponge, wet the whole of the platter to enable the paints to flow across the surface in readiness for the next step.

YOU WILL NEED

Ceramic platter or pizza plate

Large wash brush or sponge

Oven-bake enamel glaze such as Porcelaine 150 paints in abyss blue 41 (very dark blue) and anthracite 42 (black)

Nos 1 and 6 paintbrushes

Old tile or plate, for mixing paint

Small bowl of water

Kitchen paper towels

VARIATIONS

This is a perfect method for painting tiles for a splash back or a whole bathroom if you are feeling ambitious! As long as you use oven-bake paints they will stand up well to frequent washing.

2 Using a no 6 brush, apply a watery wash of the two colors, mixing them loosely together and using the side of the brush. Keep the brush moving all the time to produce an interesting base for the rest of the pattern. Leave a small amount of white in some areas as this will add contrast to the effect.

3 Mix a slightly thicker wash of the two colors and continue working into the darker areas of the design. Do not put too much color on your brush, and again, keep the brush moving all the time to create an irregular effect.

4 Continue to build up the effect by intensifying the natural characteristic effect that marble has. Remember that the pattern should be random rather than a repeating design. Use the side of the brush to achieve the natural, graded look.

5 Now, using mainly the very deep blue paint and the no 1 brush, continue to add definition until you are completely happy with the result. Once you are, leave the platter to dry for 24 hours, then bake following the manufacturer's instructions.

CLEMATIS DISH

This pretty dish looks good filled with fruit, vegetables or salad but would work equally well as a stylish bathroom accessory holding soaps or shells. We have made it deceptively easy to copy.

1 Wash the bowl in hot soapy water. We have painted seven flowers but you can change this number to suit the size of your bowl. The easiest way to divide it up accurately is to run some masking tape around the rim and cut it to the exact circumference. Then lay it out, measure it and divide by seven, then mark the spacing on the tape. Place the tape back around the bowl and make a mark with the chinagraph pencil for the position of each flower. Remove the tape.

YOU WILL NEED

Bowl
Masking tape
Ruler
Chinagraph pencil
Scissors
Oven-bake enamel glaze such as Porcelaine 150 paints in lapis blue 16, abyss blue 41(very dark blue) and bronze 28 (leaf green)
Plate for mixing the colors
No 4 brush
Small bowl of water
Kitchen paper towels
Template (see page 72)
Cotton swabs
Angle tipped brush (1 cm or ⅜ in)

VARIATIONS

Create a two-color saw tooth edging by painting alternate brush strokes in a different color. Try yellow and blue and paint the flowers on the outside the opposite color. See the Getting Started section for further details.

2 Pour a little of the two shades of blue on the mixing plate and start painting the petals using two brush strokes per petal. Using the pattern as a guide, paint five petals for each flower using the lapis blue on its own for some of them, and a mix of the two shades for other petals to create depth of color. Work on the center of the dish only at this stage and once all the steps have been completed, start on the outside.

3 Next, using the leaf green paint and the no 4 brush, link the flowers with the stalk and tendril design using a very free flowing technique. Use the pattern provided as guide.

4 Use the abyss blue and the no 4 brush or a cotton swab to make a number of small dots on the center of each flower. Use the cotton swab to remove the tiny chinagraph marks to ensure good adhesion of the paint once the dish is baked.

5 Finally, load the angle tipped brush with the lapis blue to create the saw tooth edge to the bowl making each brush stroke about 1 cm (⅜ in) long. Allow the bowl to dry for several hours before repeating the whole process on the outside, reversing the pattern. Note that the tendril design is reversed to give the bowl balance. Allow the bowl to dry completely for 24 hours, then bake following manufacturer's instructions.

FLORAL FINGER PLATES

Protect the woodwork of your doors with these finger plates decorated with a stylish design of lilies. You could also adapt this design quite easily to paint matching ceramic door knobs.

1 Wash the finger plate in hot soapy water. Mix up a pale cream background (or one to match your own decor) from the matt medium, ivory and yellow. When you are happy with the shade, sponge it evenly all over the surface. Allow it to dry, ideally for 24 hours, then bake following manufacturer's instructions. This means that mistakes are easily rectified in the next steps and you can relax as you paint!

YOU WILL NEED

Ceramic finger plate
Oven-bake enamel glaze such as Porcelaine 150 paints in matt medium, ivory 43, citrine yellow 01, amber 36, anthracite 42 (black) and bronze 28 (leaf green)
Sponge
No 1 rigger paintbrush
Small bowl of water
Kitchen paper towels
Template (see page 73)
Tracing paper
Pencil
Masking tape

VARIATIONS

Co-ordinate finger plates to your own decor by using designs from your wallpaper or borders. Remember you cannot sell any work copied in this way but it is fine for your own use and gives the room a co-ordinated look.

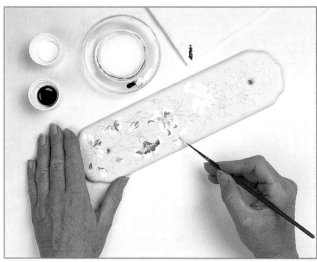

2 The finger plate now has a smooth, matt surface which is easy to work on and takes the paint well. Trace the pattern provided using the pencil. Turn the tracing over and position it centrally on the finger plate. Tape it in position before carefully drawing over all the lines, thus transferring the design to the plate.

3 The lilies are painted first using the ivory, and then the darker areas added by mixing the ivory with a touch of black. Use very delicate brush strokes and make some areas slightly darker to add shadows. Paint the buds in the same way.

4 Build up a base of green stems and leaves by using the green in a variety of mixes with the black and white to create depth to the design. Allow the green to dry before being tempted to move on to the next stage.

5 Finally, add very fine stamens using the same brush and light brush strokes. Allow the finger plate to dry for 24 hours, then bake following the manufacturer's instructions.

STARRY BREAKFAST CUP AND SAUCER

Just the thing to fill with hot milky coffee for a lazy breakfast, or even a hearty soup on a cold winter's night! This idea could easily be adapted to use on something of lesser proportions – simply reduce the size of the templates on a photocopier.
Less dramatically, the design would work equally well on plain white china.

1 Wash the cup and saucer in hot soapy water. Using the gold paint, lightly sponge around the edge of the cup and saucer, allowing the gold to fade out with a slightly uneven finish. Leave them to dry for a few hours before continuing with the next step.

YOU WILL NEED

Large cup and saucer
Sponge
Oven-bake enamel glaze such as Porcelaine 150 in gold 44
Paper
Scissors
Template (see page 72)
Aerosol glue
Oven-bake enamel glaze outliner in gold
Kitchen paper towels
Scalpel or toothpick

—— VARIATIONS ——
This design would look good around the edge of a serving bowl brimming over with festive treats!

2 Copy a number of both sizes of stars onto paper, cut out and lightly spray with glue on the back. Position the stars around the cup alternating between large and small to create a random effect.

3 If you have not used outliners before, it is a good idea to practice first. Have a piece of kitchen paper to hand to catch any blobs before you begin start outlining the stars. Use the templates as a guide only and make sure that the outliner does not touch them. Allow the outliner to dry for several hours before being tempted to remove the paper shapes with the scalpel or toothpick.

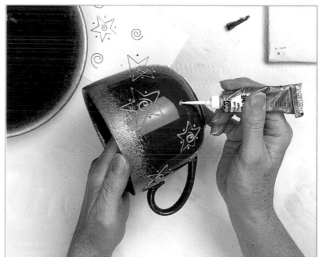

4 Use the template as a guide to add the dots and whirls to the center of each star. Carefully tidy up any uneven paint with a scalpel.

5 Finally, fill in the gaps between each star with the whirl motif. Alternatively, you could use a different design at this stage such as groups of three dots or crosses. Allow to dry for 24 hours, then bake following manufacturer's instructions.

TILES GALLERY

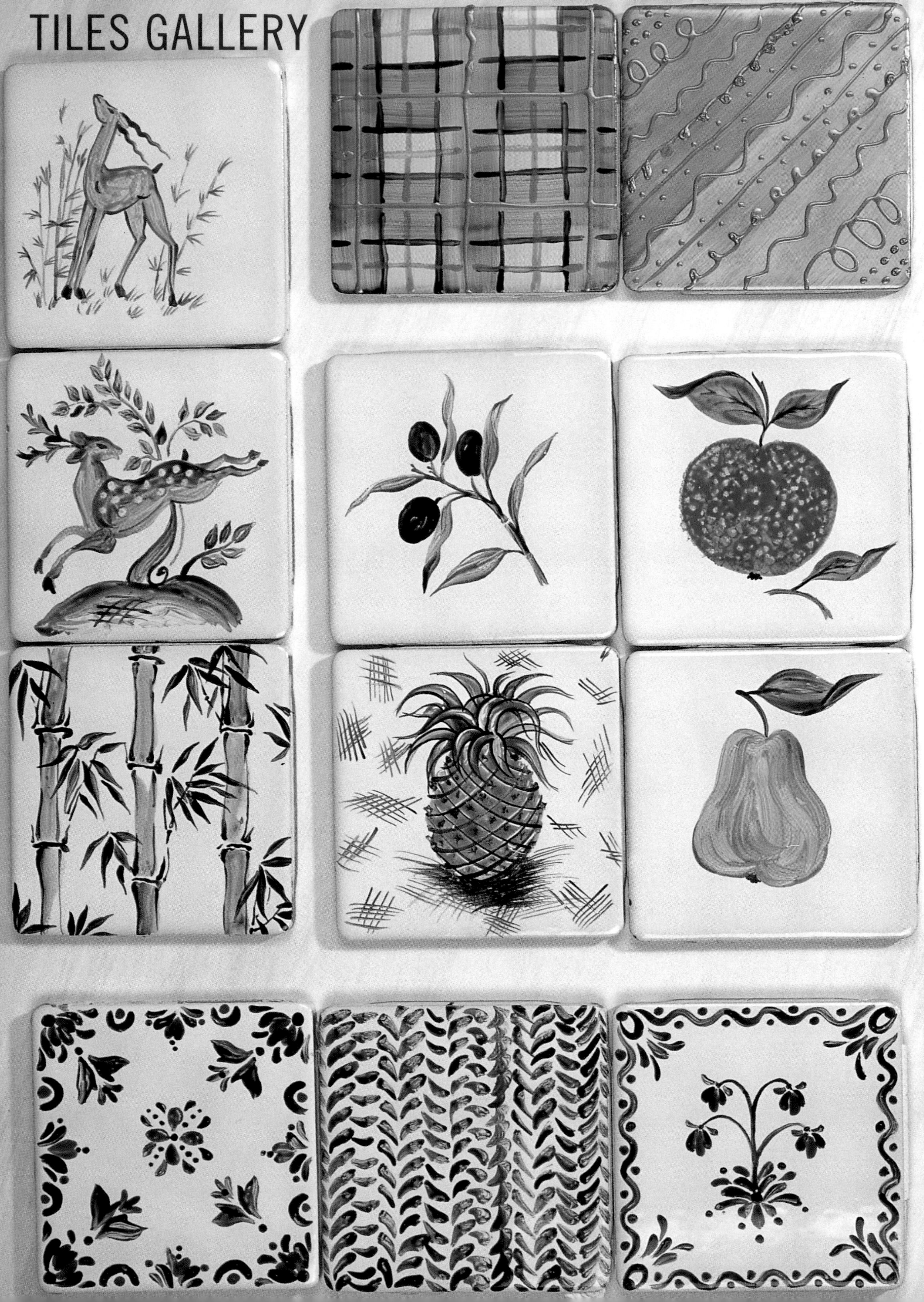

FISH TILES

Plain tiles destined for the bathroom or kitchen wall can easily be decorated with ceramic paint. Once baked, they can be wiped clean using a damp cloth and non-abrasive cleaning fluid. This is a very easy project – you can either work freehand or use the template provided. We have painted two fish, but to build up a larger tableau, paint the fish swimming in different directions on a selection of tiles.

1 Wash the tiles in hot soapy water. Lay out all the tiles you want to decorate, but only work on one at a time as the paint dries very quickly. Using the 2 cm (¾ in) wash brush and emerald green, paint four wavy lines down the first tile.

YOU WILL NEED

Fish template (see page 74)

White ceramic tiles

Oven-bake enamel glaze such as Porcelaine 150 paints in emerald green 19, Ming blue 17 and abyss blue 41

2 cm (¾ in) wash brush

No 1 paintbrush

Kitchen paper towels

Small bowl of water

Toothpick

TIP

Save any slightly chipped or cracked tiles for practicing the brush techniques.

VARIATIONS

We have teamed our fish tiles with a really simple, wide striped design. The fine line was added last. Just imagine how different the same design would look painted in yellows and oranges with golden highlights. Experiment with color!

2 While the paint is still wet, fill in the gaps with the Ming blue to produce a wavy effect. Blend the color slightly as you go in order to produce a more natural, watery effect.

3 It is a good idea to practice painting the fish several times on a spare plain tile first to get a really flowing look. Once you are confident, paint each fish with Ming blue using two simple brush strokes as shown. Either do this freehand or use the template as a guide.

4 Define the outline of the fish using the fine paintbrush and the abyss blue to create a smooth, continuous line. Add fin and gill details using the template as a guide. Finally, add a few bubbles to the background and wavy lines to simulate the movement of the water.

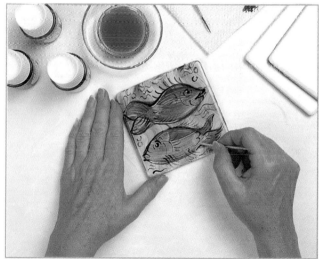

5 To further define and emphasize the fish shape, use a toothpick to scrape the paint off parts of the outline. If you are not happy with the result, repaint the outline with abyss blue and repeat. Allow to dry for 24 hours and then bake according to manufacturer's instructions.

MEXICAN-STYLE LAMP BASE

The combination of five toning shades of warm browns and gold combine to produce this magnificent patchwork of color. Although it looks very impressive, it is easy enough for a beginner to tackle.

1 If you are using oven-bake paints as we have, it is important to remove all the wiring first. Then wash the base thoroughly in hot soapy water before you begin. Use the masking tape to mask off areas at random but leaving shapes large enough to decorate.

YOU WILL NEED

Ceramic lamp base
Masking tape
Scissors
Oven-bake enamel glaze such as Porcelaine 150 paints in amber 36, calcite 35, mummy brown 39 (dark brown), esterel 37, Havana 34 and gold 44 (if you are using another brand of paint, mix up a selection of shades of browns)
Sponge
2 cm (¾ in) flat wash brush
1 cm (⅜ in) angle tipped paint brush
Small bowl of water
Kitchen paper towels
Sheet of cellophane
Cotton swabs

— VARIATIONS —

There are a number of design ideas here which may easily be used to transform a set of coffee cups. Each one could be slightly different or an alternative selection of colors.

2 Sponge the exposed areas of the lamp base with a selection of shades. We have used all the colors listed at this stage, but you could use just one or two colors if you prefer. Allow the base to dry for a few hours before carrying on. Carefully peel away the masking tape and clean up any messy areas before continuing.

3 Now, using the wide wash brush and smooth continuous strokes, fill in the white areas with the esterel paint. Allow the paint to dry for another 20 minutes or so and then add some narrower lines with the angled brush and the dark brown.

4 Experiment with brush strokes on a piece of cellophane as we have to create various textural designs. We used herringbone, basketweave effect and circles which only require simple strokes. Use a variety of these effects on the sponged areas of the lamp base.

5 Finally, add further embellishment to the design with stitch effect brush strokes in gold, and add dark brown spots by dipping a cotton swab into the brown paint. Allow the base to dry for 24 hours, then bake following the manufacturer's instructions and reassemble the lamp.

CHECKERED VASE

Just imagine this vase sitting on a sunny windowsill brimming over with colorful sunflowers or cheerful gerbera! We have worked out an exceptionally easy way to apply the color evenly in case your painting skills are still rather shaky.

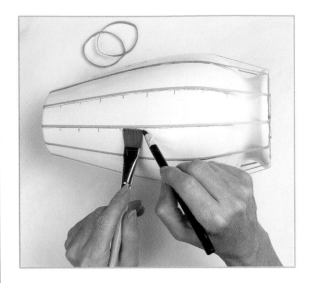

1 Wash the vase in hot soapy water. Taking one rubber band at a time, stretch it around the vase, making sure that it lies flat and is even. The number of bands used will determine the width of the checks. When you are happy with the spacing, make tiny marks the width of the wash brush with the chinagraph pencil along the side of each band.

YOU WILL NEED

Vase
Large rubber bands, all the same size
Wide flat wash brush 2 cm (¾ in)
Chinagraph pencil
Oven-bake enamel glaze such as Porcelaine 150 paints in citrine 01, olive 27, marseille yellow 02 and emerald 19
Small bowl of water
Kitchen paper towels
Cotton swabs
Fine liner paintbrush

VARIATIONS

Try masking off a large area on the front of the vase while you paint the checks. Later, remove the mask and fill the area with a single large flower head in yellow or gold to complement the pot. Experiment with other colors for the fine lines too.

2 With the wide wash brush and using the grid as a guide only, paint wide bands of orange randomly around the vase, filling about a quarter of the spaces. Try to avoid letting any of the paint go over the chinagraph lines which are there as a guide only.

3 Continue to build up the checks, using the other colors, again placing them randomly around the vase until all the spaces are painted. Use each color to fill about a quarter of the spaces. It is a good idea to allow the paint to dry for a few hours before moving on to the next step.

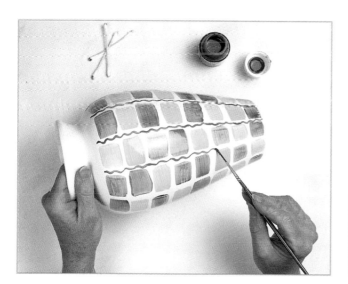

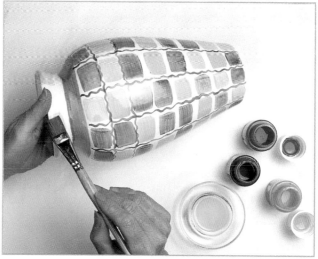

4 Use cotton swabs to remove the chinagraph lines completely. With the fine liner brush, apply the emerald green in long wavy lines both vertically and horizontally to create a grid around the colored blocks.

5 Complete the vase by painting bands of color around the top with the wide brush using the photograph as a guide. Add a band of emerald to delineate the colors. Allow the vase to dry for 24 hours, then bake following the manufacturer's instructions.

CHERRY COFFEE CUPS

Here is a delightfully simple way of cheering up a set of plain white coffee cups and saucers. We have just used cherries to decorate our set, but apples, oranges, lemons or pears would look just as good, as would a variety of different colored backgrounds.

1 Wash the china in hot soapy water. Work out the size of 'window' you would like on the front of each cup. Ours are 28 x 25 mm (1⅛ x 1 in). As this idea would also work well on coffee mugs, the whole design can be enlarged. Cut a paper mask for the front and back of each cup and use the glue to hold it lightly in place.

YOU WILL NEED

Coffee cups and saucers
Paper
Pencil
Ruler
Scissors
Spray mount or glue stick
Oven-bake enamel glaze such as Porcelaine 150 paints in parma violet 14, bronze 28 (leaf green) and etruscan red 12 (maroon)
Template (see page 74)
Sponge
Small bowl of water
No 1 paintbrush
Scalpel
Oven-bake enamel glaze outliner in gold

VARIATIONS

Instead of sponging around the window stencil, you could paint colorful stripes or bands of color. The more confident you are, the more adventurous your ideas and design will become. Remember, it is easy to wash the paint off and start again!

2 Now, using the fine sponge and the parma violet, apply the paint evenly over the entire surface working quickly as the paint dries very fast when sponged on. Leave the center of the saucer plain.

3 Remove the mask and clean up any rough edges if necessary. Remove any residue of glue that may remain on. Using the pattern as a guide, paint the leaves and stalks green with smooth, even brush strokes.

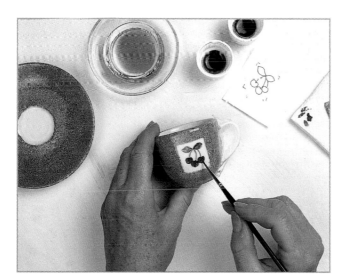

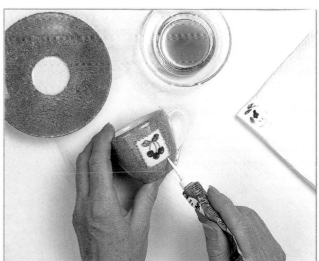

4 Now paint the cherries with the rich etruscan red and put the cups on one side to dry completely before continuing. Part-bake at this stage if you wish.

5 Finally, use the outliner to add neat dots all around the outside of the 'window'. You will see from the main photograph that we have also used straight lines which overlap at both ends as well as a corkscrew design. Allow to dry for 24 hours, then bake following the manufacturer's instructions.

EGG CUPS GALLERY

PLAYING CARD EGG CUPS

Sponging the gold into the insides of these plain white egg cups makes them look very luxurious but is quick and simple to do. This attractive design could also be adapted to decorate tableware or ceramic storage jars.

1 Wash the egg cups in hot soapy water. Use a tiny piece of sponge to apply a coat of gold paint to the inside of each egg cup and to the bottom outer edges. Leave the egg cups to dry and repeat if necessary until the gold reaches the required density.

YOU WILL NEED

Set of egg cups, any size
Sponge
No 4 paintbrush
Oven-bake enamel glaze such as Porcelaine 150 paints in gold 44, and ruby 07
Oven-bake enamel glaze outliner in gold
Scissors
String
Chinagraph pencil
Template (see page 74)
Sheet of cellophane
Kitchen paper towels
Small bowl of water

VARIATIONS

Why not paint matching side plates to stand the egg cups on? We painted all our suits red but of course you may prefer to paint the spades and clubs true to form in black. See the egg cup gallery for other ideas.

2 In order to space the motifs equally, you will need to mark the egg cup using the chinagraph pencil. We found that the easiest way to do this is to cut a length of string to fit around the rim, then simply fold it into four, marking it with the chinagraph and then transferring the markings onto the egg cups.

3 We have provided templates for you to copy onto the egg cups. There are several ways you can do this. The simplest is to practice on cellophane with the pattern underneath or as we have done here, simply using the pattern as a guide. When you feel confident with your work, transfer the suits onto the egg cups. You could cut stencils and sponge the design on if you wish.

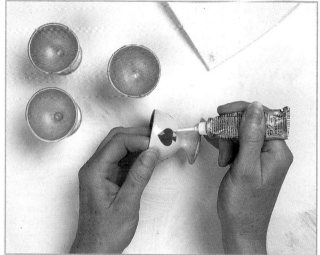

4 Now start working directly onto the egg cups using the no 4 brush and allowing the paint to flow quite thickly for a really good depth of color.

5 Once the motifs have had several hours to dry, use the outliner to apply dots evenly around the edge of each one. Leave to dry for 24 hours and then stand the egg cups on a plate before baking them following the manufacturer's instructions.

CHECKERED FRUIT PLATES

These bright and colorful plates are fun, easy to paint and are perfect to use for serving fruit on at the end of a meal. We have painted just three fruits, but there are many other fruits or vegetables you could add to the range.

1 Wash the china in hot soapy water. Start by painting two wide blue bands around the outer rim of the plate using the wash brush as shown. Do not worry if your painting is a bit uneven as this will add to its rustic charm. Leave the plate to dry for about 20 minutes.

YOU WILL NEED

Side plates
2 cm (¾ in) wash brush
Nos 6 and 2 paintbrushes
Sponge
'Spoke' template (see page 75)
Oven-bake enamel glaze such as Porcelaine 150 paints in lapis 16 (bright blue), agate 04 (orange), bronze 28 (leaf green), scarlet 06 and mummy brown 39 (dark brown)
Toothpick or rubber shaper brush
Kitchen paper towels
Small bowl of water

--- **TIP** ---

For perfect circles on the edge of the plate, use an old record player! See page 11 for further details.

--- **VARIATIONS** ---

Try painting cherries in a rich burgundy color with purple edging or for something really spectacular, paint the fruits in gold, and band the plates with black.

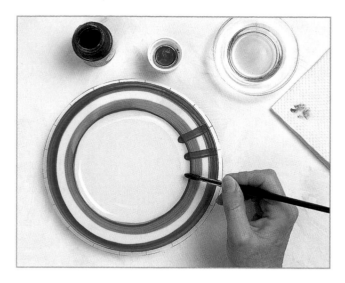

2 Lay the plate over the 'spoke' template and using the no 6 brush, paint from inside the rim outwards towards the edge using the template as a guide for spacing. Alternatively, paint the spokes freehand leaving a gap of about 1 cm (⅜ in) between them.

3 Gather up a small piece of sponge into a round ball and use this to sponge the orange. Work from the center outwards, dabbing the sponge with a circular motion to achieve the peel effect. If the paint is applied unevenly, the orange will appear to have more depth.

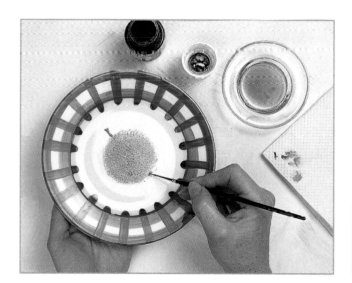

4 Use the no 2 brush and the dark brown to paint in the stalk and to add a tiny bit of detail to the bottom of the orange to make it look more realistic.

5 Finally, paint the leaf with the no 2 brush and green paint, allowing the paint to flow more thickly near the edges. Immediately etch in the detail of the leaf veins using the shaper brush or toothpick. Leave the plate to dry completely for 24 hours, then bake following manufacturer's instructions.

ANEMONE PLATE

Enjoy the beauty of these gorgeous flowers all year round by reproducing them on a plate as we have done. The secret is to use as many intense yet harmonious colors as possible – the larger your palette of colors the better. A set of eight with matching side plates would make a unique designer dinner service.

1 Wash the plate in hot soapy water. Copy the pattern onto the tracing paper and cut it out. Tape the tracing upside down onto the plate to hold it in place while you carefully draw over the lines in order to transfer the design onto the plate. Alternatively, use a coin to rub the design onto the plate. The result is a faint outline which will help you to place the flowers.

YOU WILL NEED

Dinner plate – ours is 28 cm (11 in)
Template (see page 76)
Tracing or greaseproof paper
Pencil
Scissors
Masking tape
Coin
No 6 paintbrush
Oven-bake enamel glaze such as Porcelaine 150 paints in scarlet 06, ruby 07, azurite 15 (purple), amethyst 13, bronze 28 (leaf green) and etruscan 12 (maroon)
Kitchen paper towels

VARIATIONS

If your palette of colors is very limited, why not paint all the flowers bright red to imitate poppies instead. They usually have four or five petals and similar centers. Use a photograph of real poppies in order to copy the leaves.

2 Now start painting the red flowers first, working from the outer edge of each petal towards the center. Use simple, flowing brush strokes and avoid laboring over each flower.

3 Continue to paint the rest of the flowers with the different shades of reds and mauves, working quickly to keep the whole design fresh and spontaneous. It is best to allow the plate to dry for an hour or so before continuing with the leaves.

4 Imitate the frond-like leaves and stems by using the no 2 brush and the leaf green. We have not given a pattern for the leaves as they are simple to paint with single brush strokes. Fill in the white areas between the flowers, building up the density until you are happy with the result.

5 Finally, add the dark centers using the no 2 brush and the black paint. Start by painting the large central areas and then add a few random dots around each one. Allow the plate to dry for a full 24 hours before being tempted to bake it following the manufacturer's instructions.

HERB-EDGED FISH PLATTER

This elegant fish platter looks so good with its decorative border of garden herbs, but just one word of warning if you would like to copy it – do make sure it will fit in your oven first!

1 Wash the plate in hot soapy water. Trace off the pattern for the two herbs using a fairly soft pencil and cut around the tracing fairly close to the edge. Turn the tracing over and then tape it into place around the edge of the platter once you have decided the position of the herbs. Use a coin to rub gently over the back of the tracing in order to transfer the pattern to the platter.

YOU WILL NEED

Long fish platter
Template (see page 77)
Tracing paper
Soft pencil, 5b for example
Scissors
Masking tape
Coin
Oven-bake enamel glaze such as Porcelaine 150 paints in green-gold 31, amazonite 29 (dark green), bronze 28 (leaf green), azurite 15 (purple), petrol 22 (blue-black), olive green 27 and ivory 43
Fine liner brush
Old tile or plate, for mixing paints and to practice on
Small bowl of water
Kitchen paper towels

VARIATIONS

If you are feeling ambitious, why not edge the platter with a whole range of different herbs instead of just two. Use a reference book or fresh herbs for inspiration.

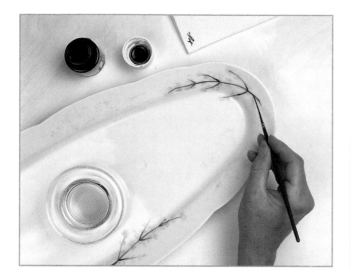

2 Paint the stems of the thyme with the green-gold using a fine liner brush. Use long sweeping movements for a more natural effect. It may be an idea to have a practice run on an old plate or tile until you feel sufficiently confident. The design can be as complicated or as stylized as you wish.

3 The thyme leaves are painted with a mix of the three greens and petrol blue to add a realistic look to them. Dip your brush in and out of the four colors without mixing them and this will give the natural effect of light and shade.

4 Now paint the stems, leaves and buds on the summer savory with the olive green paint mixed with a little dark green. Work quickly and freely for a painterly effect.

5 The flowers are painted with azurite and ivory, again not mixing the two colors together but simply dipping the brush from one color into the other so that the flowers appear to have more depth to them. Allow the dish to dry for 24 hours, then bake following the manufacturer's instructions.

SPANISH-STYLE PLANTER

A few simple brush strokes are all that is needed to create this eye-catching planter. It is a free technique and the flowers are simply painted on at random.

1 Wash the pot in hot soapy water. This is such a free technique we have applied it straight onto the pot without prior marking. If you do not feel sufficiently confident, use a pencil to mark faint outlines of the flowers. The petals are made up of three brush strokes, each working from the outside towards the center of each one with a no 6 paintbrush. Paint all the pink flowers first and then go back over them working more color into the center of each one. Allow the flowers to flow over the top rim. It is best to allow the pot to dry before moving on to the next step.

YOU WILL NEED

Ceramic pot

Template (see page 77)

Nos 6 and 2 paintbrushes

Oven-bake enamel glaze such as Porcelaine 150 paints in garnet 11, amber 36, peridot green 30 (olive), and mummy brown 39 (very dark brown)

Kitchen paper towels

Small bowl of water

VARIATIONS

Once you have mastered the idea of painting these flowers, you can make them larger or smaller depending on the size of your object. Scaled down, this would make a stunning set of coffee mugs and each one could be a different color scheme.

2 Repeat the process as before but this time using the amber paint and fill in the spaces between the pink flowers already painted and go over the top edge as before. Again, allow the pot to dry before proceeding.

3 The background color is also painted using the no 6 brush and the peridot green. The stippled effect is achieved by applying the paint with quick, short brush strokes. Fill in all the white areas between the flowers but remember that precision is not important with this style of painting.

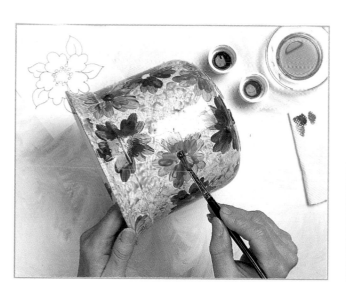

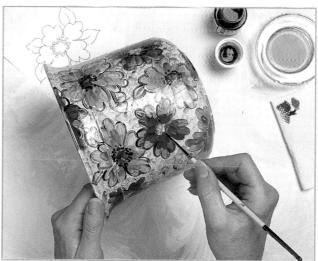

4 Paint the centers of the flowers by using the amber in the center of the garnet flowers and vice versa. Use the no 6 brush and a stippling movement to give the appearance of stamens.

5 Finally, outline the petals of each flower using the no 2 brush and the dark brown. Use the template as a rough guide to paint the flower centers and then add a few leaves where there are spaces to fit them in.

FIFTIES-STYLE COFFEE POT

Reproduce the classic, simple lines and colors of this era with the sheer simplicity of this project. This elegant design also translates well onto plates and cups and saucers, so you could paint a complete set of matching china.

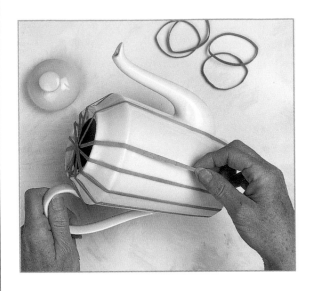

1 Wash the pot in hot soapy water. Then take the rubber bands and wrap them equidistantly around the pot as shown in order to create even vertical lines.

YOU WILL NEED

Coffee pot
Large rubber bands of equal size
Ruler
Chinagraph pencil
Scissors
Oven-bake enamel glaze such as Porcelaine 150 paint in anthracite 42 (black)
No 4 paintbrush
Hairdryer (optional)
Oven-bake enamel glaze outliner in gold
Old tile or plate
Small bowl of water
Kitchen paper towels

— VARIATIONS —

Paint coffee cups and saucers, milk jug and sugar bowl to match. Combining red and gold would be very festive with a holly leaf pattern substituted for the gold swirls.

2 Mark the center of each band with a chinagraph pencil. This will make it easier to position and paint the three black areas as shown. Allow the paint to dry before carefully removing the rubber bands. A hairdryer will speed up this process if you are impatient!

3 Paint more black areas between the first ones to create a checkerboard effect as shown and again allow the paint to dry thoroughly before moving on to the next stage.

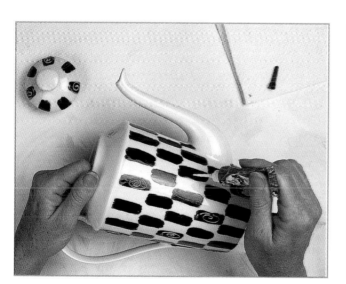

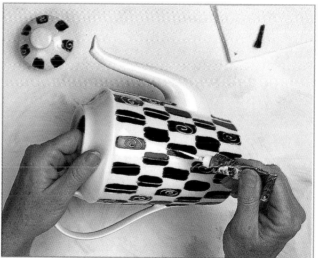

4 Use the outliner to apply the swirls to some of the black areas. It is a good idea to practice this on an old tile or plate first in order to perfect your technique. Have a piece of paper towel close to hand in order to keep the nozzle clean.

5 Now use the outliner to make vertical lines on some of the other black areas, remembering to leave some of them unembellished. Finish the lid too and allow them both to dry for 24 hours, then bake following the manufacturer's instructions.

ESPRESSO COFFEE CUPS

This simple, white set of cups and saucers in a traditional shape has been elevated to designer status with the addition of a little ceramic paint and some imagination. The dotted line in gold outliner provides the perfect finishing touch to after-dinner coffee cups.

1 Wash the china in hot soapy water. Before you start, it is a good idea to have a trial run at painting the scallop edging directly onto a saucer, as it is quite easy to do freehand with a little practice. Alternatively, use the scallop design as a guide and draw the outline with the chinagraph pencil onto the inner and outer rims of the cups and saucers as shown. Do not feel that you have to stick to the scale we have used. If you feel happier painting larger scallops, then do so but remember it will be more difficult to make them meet up neatly.

YOU WILL NEED

| Set of coffee cups and saucers |
| Nos 1 and 2 paintbrushes |
| Template (see page 74) |
| Chinagraph pencil |
| Oven-bake enamel glaze such as Porcelaine 150 paints in mummy brown 39 (very dark brown), esterel 37 (burnt sienna) and gold 44 |
| Oven-bake enamel glaze outliner in gold |
| Small bowl of water |
| Kitchen paper towels |

--- VARIATIONS ---

Why not enlarge the design to create a matching dinner service?
Experiment with different color combinations too.

2 Next, using the fine paintbrush, carefully fill in the outline with the dark brown. Work around all the cups and saucers, remembering to fill in both the inner and outer rims of both.

3 Using the burnt sienna paint and the fine brush, paint the motif of a set of three lines with a central dot under alternate scallops. You will notice that this part of the design is mirrored to balance the depth of the cup, but not on the saucer.

4 Continue to follow the pattern by adding the gold details to the cups as shown, again using a fine brush and steady hand.

5 Finally, using the gold outliner, add fine dots to the design to add another dimension to the surface. Allow the crockery to dry for 24 hours before baking following manufacturer's instructions.

TEMPLATES

The templates shown here are actual size. They may be easily enlarged or reduced on a photocopier to suit the size of the item you wish to decorate.

Colorwashed cookie jar

(see page 20)

Barge-ware pot
(see page 22)

Jazz jug
(see page 26)

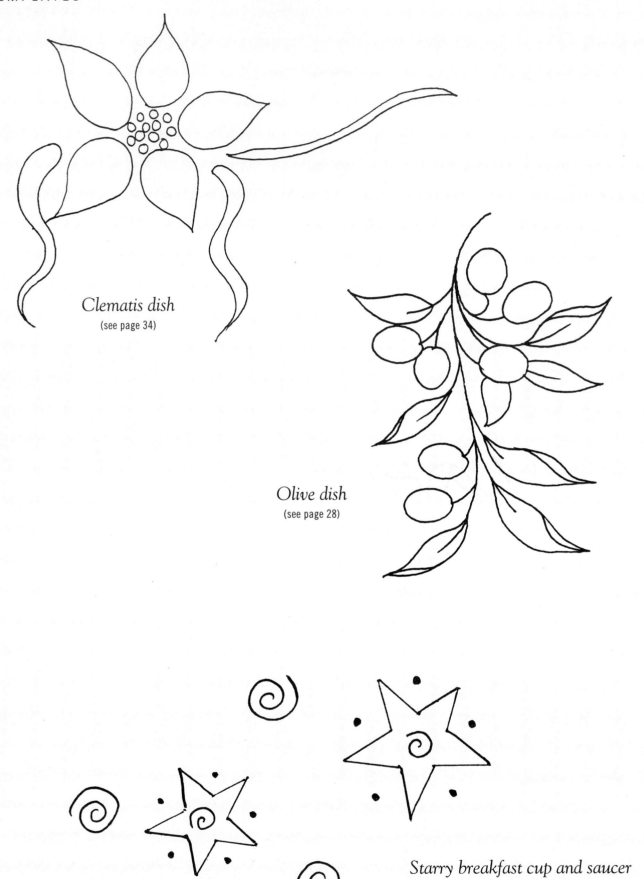

Clematis dish
(see page 34)

Olive dish
(see page 28)

Starry breakfast cup and saucer
(see page 38)

Floral finger plates
(see page 36)

Cherry coffee cups
(see page 48)

Espresso coffee cups
(see page 68)

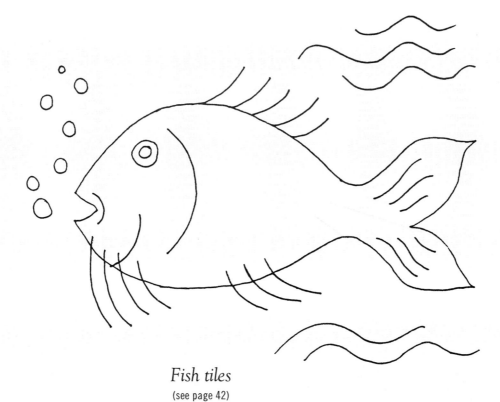

Fish tiles
(see page 42)

   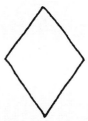

Playing card egg cups
(see page 52)

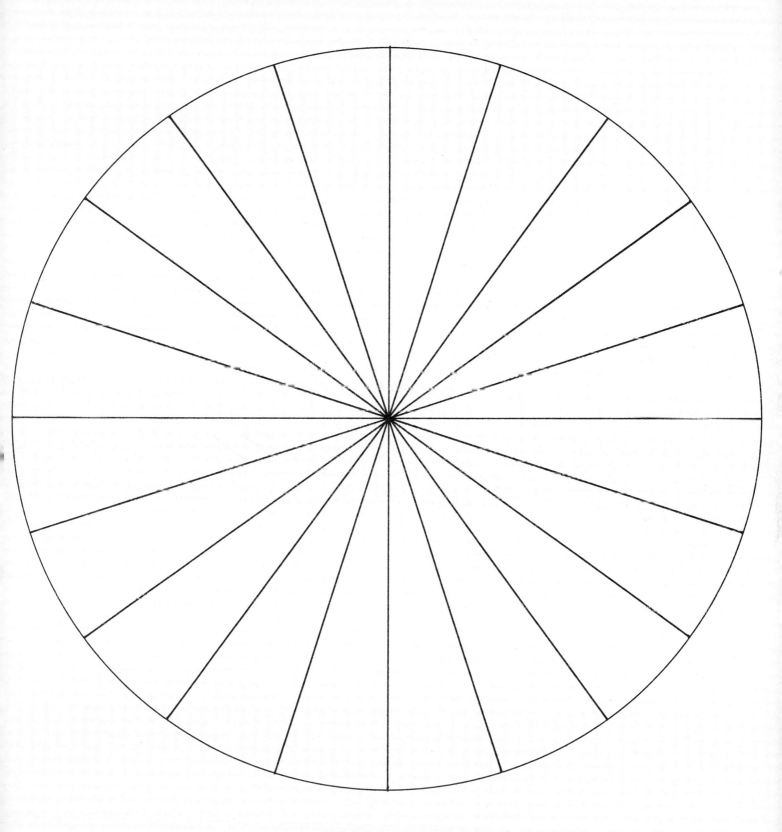

Checkered fruit plates
(see page 54)

Anemone plate
(see page 58)
Enlarge this template on a photocopier
to 140% to fit a plate with a diameter
of 28 cm (11 in).

Herb-edged fish platter
(see page 60)

Spanish-style planter
(see page 62)

SUPPLIERS

UNITED STATES & CANADA

The Art Store
4004 Hillsboro Pike
Nashville, TN 37215
Tel: (800) 999-4601
Website: http://www.artstoreplus.com
(Pébéo paints and outliners plus
 other surface design products)

Dick Blick Art Materials
P. O. Box 1267
Galesburg, IL 61402-1267
Tel: (800) 828-4548
(Pébéo paints and art supplies)

Home Craft
P. O. Box 24890
San Jose, CA 95154-4890
Tel: (800) 301-7377
(Pébéo paints and craft supplies)

Pearl Paint
308 Canal Street
New York City, NY 10013
Tel: (800) 221-6845
Website: http://www.pearlpaint.com
(Pébéo paints, rubber shaper brushes,
 chinagraph pencils, full range of art supplies)

Pébéo of America, Inc.
Airport Road, P.O. Box 714
Swanton, VT 05488
Tel: (800) 363-5012

Pébéo Canada
1905 Roy Street
Sherbrooke, Quebec, CAN
J1K 2X5
Tel: (819) 829-5012

Pébéo Website: http://www.pebeo.com
(Manufacturer of Porcelaine 150 paints.
 Check out their website or call for a distributer near you.)

Stained Glass Studio
4433 Chastant Street
Metairie, LA 70006
Tel: (504) 889-0225
(Pébéo paints and other surface decoration
 products for ceramics and glass)

Sunshine Craft Distributors
12335, 62nd Street North
Largo, FL 33773
Tel: (800) 729-2878
(Pébéo paints and art supplies)

ACKNOWLEDGEMENTS

We would like to say a very big thank you to Paul
Sparrow of F. Trauffler Ltd who has generously
provided elegant white china by leading French
manufacturers, Apilco, for us to embellish.
Thanks to Pébéo UK, in particular John Wright,
for their abundant supply of paints and outliners
and to Carol Hook of Clear Communications for
her help. We were delighted with the rubber
shaper brushes provided by Forsline and Starr as
they are perfect for etching details in the paints.

Finally, to Tony and Jim for putting up with us,
our mess, our moods and our mountains of china
salvaged from every local bootsale causing shelves
to sag and cupboard doors not to shut – thank
you very much indeed!

INDEX